The Way of the Cross
for Children

By Rev. Jude Winkler, OFM Conv.

Imprimi Potest: Mark Curesky, OFM Conv., Minister Provincial of St. Anthony of Padua Province (USA)
Nihil Obstat: James T. O'Connor, S.T.D., Censor Librorum
Imprimatur: ✠ Patrick J. Sheridan, D.D., Vicar General, Archdiocese of New York

The Nihil Obstat and Imprimatur are official declarations that a book or pamphlet is free of doctrinal or moral error. No implication is contained therein that those who have granted the Nihil Obstat and Imprimatur agree with the contents, opinions or statements expressed.

FIRST STATION

Jesus Is Condemned to Death

Leader: We adore You, O Christ, and we bless You.

All: Because by Your holy Cross You have redeemed the world.

THE leaders of the people brought Jesus before Pilate, the Roman governor. He wanted to set Jesus free, but the people demanded that Jesus be put to death. Pilate washed his hands to show he was not guilty of the blood of Jesus, and then he sent Him out to be nailed to the Cross.

LET us pray.
Jesus, You so loved us that,
even though You were innocent,
You allowed Yourself to be
condemned to death.
May we follow Your example
and reject every kind of selfishness
that might lead us away from You.

All:

**JESUS,
please teach us Your love.
Never let us be
like the people who hurt You,
or even like Pilate,
who did nothing to help You.
Teach us to love
and to help all people.
Amen.**

Hymn:

**At the Cross her station keeping
Stood the mournful Mother weeping,
Close to Jesus to the last.**

SECOND STATION

Jesus Takes Up His Cross

Leader: We adore You, O Christ, and we bless You.

All: Because by Your holy Cross You have redeemed the world.

THE soldiers treated Jesus with great cruelty. They beat Him and placed a crown of thorns on His head. Now they led Him outside and placed the wood of the Cross on His shoulder. They made Him carry the Cross as they led Him to the place where He would die.

L ET us pray.
Jesus,
even though the Cross was heavy
and You were weak and tired,
You still took up Your Cross
out of love for us.
Teach all of us to carry our crosses
out of love for You.

All:

J ESUS,
You have taught us
that when we love people,
we are willing to help them,
even if it hurts.
Give us the courage
to help our family and friends,
even if that means we must give up
something we really wanted.
Amen.

Hymn:

Through her heart, His sorrow sharing,
All His bitter anguish bearing,
Lo, the piercing sword has passed!

THIRD STATION

Jesus Falls the First Time

Leader: We adore You, O Christ, and we bless You.

All: Because by Your holy Cross You have redeemed the world.

JESUS had not been allowed to sleep all night, and He was now exhausted. He had been beaten and whipped, and He was nearing the end of His strength. Even as He tried to walk along, the soldiers continued to push and shove Him. Finally, it was too much for Him and He fell down.

Leader:

LET us pray.
Jesus,
when You were born in Bethlehem,
You took our weakness upon Yourself.
Grant that we may always
look to You as the source
of our strength.

All:

**JESUS,
You became weak and fell down in pain.
Teach us never to make fun of
those who are weak
or those who have fallen.
And when we fall,
teach us to reach out to You.
Amen.**

Hymn:

O, how sad and sore distressed
Was that Mother highly blessed
Of the sole-begotten One.

FOURTH STATION

Jesus Meets His Mother, Mary

Leader: We adore You, O Christ, and we bless You.

All: **Because by Your holy Cross You have redeemed the world.**

A S the soldiers dragged Jesus through the streets, they led Him to the place where Mary, His Mother, was standing. Mary felt such great sorrow to see her only Son suffering such horrible pain. Yet Jesus had assured her that He must fulfill the Father's will. So she surrendered her Son to the will of the Father.

LET us pray.
Jesus,
when You were dying,
You told Your beloved disciple
to care for Mary, Your Mother.
May we, too, remember
that she is our Mother.
May we make a home for her
in our hearts.

All:

HAIL, Mary, full of grace,
the Lord is with you.
**Blessed are you among women,
and blessed is the fruit of your womb,
Jesus.
Holy Mary, Mother of God,
pray for us sinners,
now and at the hour of our death.
Amen.**

Hymn:

Christ above in torment hangs,
She beneath beholds the pangs
Of her dying glorious Son.

FIFTH STATION
Simon Helps Jesus Carry the Cross

Leader: We adore You, O Christ, and we bless You.

All: Because by Your holy Cross You have redeemed the world.

THE soldiers realized that Jesus was too weak to carry His Cross all the way to Calvary. They began to worry that He might die along the way. So they forced a man who was standing nearby, Simon of Cyrene, to carry the Cross for Jesus the rest of the way.

Leader:

LET us pray.
When Your strength failed You, Jesus,
You accepted the help of Simon of Cyrene.
May we never fear
asking for help
from our family and friends,
and especially from You!

All:

JESUS,
Simon reached out
and helped You carry the Cross.
Teach me to reach out
to help those around me.
Let me be so generous
that I offer my help even without being
  asked.
Amen.

Hymn:

Is there one who would not weep
'Whelmed in miseries so deep
Christ's dear Mother to behold?

SIXTH STATION

Veronica Wipes the Face of Jesus

Leader: We adore You, O Christ, and we bless You.

All: **Because by Your holy Cross You have redeemed the world.**

J ESUS was now totally exhausted. Many of the people around Him mocked Him and spit at Him. One courageous woman named Veronica came forward and wiped the face of Jesus with her veil. God rewarded her loving kindness, for He caused an image of the face of Jesus to appear on her veil.

LET us pray.
Jesus,
Veronica saw Your suffering,
and she put away her fears
to reach out to You in love.
Help us to put away our fears
and reach out to those
who are different in whatever way.

All:

**JESUS,
Veronica saw the pain in Your face,
and so she reached out to help You.
Remind us
that every time we see the face of someone
who is suffering or lonely,
we are really seeing You.
Amen.**

Hymn:

Can the human heart refrain
From partaking in the pain,
In that Mother's pain untold?

SEVENTH STATION

Jesus Falls the Second Time

Leader: We adore You, O Christ, and we bless You.

All: Because by Your holy Cross You have redeemed the world.

THE soldiers kept leading Jesus along, but He continued to grow weaker and weaker. Once again, His strength failed Him and He fell to the ground. The soldiers immediately forced Him to get back on His feet and to continue His cruel journey.

Leader:

L ET us pray.
Lord Jesus,
the soldiers showed You no mercy
as You grew weaker, stumbled and fell.
Grant that we may never rejoice
in the downfall of another,
even if it is someone whom we do not like.

All:

**J ESUS,
You told us that we would receive
 mercy
if we showed mercy to others.
Teach us to forgive,
even if someone has wronged us
time and time again.
Amen.**

Hymn:
Bruised, derided, cursed, defiled,
She beheld her tender Child,
All with bloody scourges rent.

EIGHTH STATION

Jesus Meets the Weeping Women

Leader: We adore You, O Christ, and we bless You.

All: Because by Your holy Cross You have redeemed the world.

A S Jesus struggled along, He encountered a group of women who were weeping for Him. He looked up and told them that they should not weep for Him, but rather for themselves and their children.

LET us pray.
Jesus,
even though You were exhausted
and were on the way to Your death,
You took time to speak to some women of
    Jerusalem.
Let us never be so busy
with what we are doing
that we ignore the needs of those around us.

All:

**JESUS,
the women wept for You
as You went off to die.
May we pray now
for all those who are dying and have died.
Eternal rest grant unto them, O Lord,
and let perpetual light
shine upon them.
Amen.**

Hymn:

**For the sins of His own nation
Saw Him hang in desolation
Till His Spirit forth He sent.**

NINTH STATION

Jesus Falls the Third Time

Leader: We adore You, O Christ, and we bless You.

All: Because by Your holy Cross You have redeemed the world.

JESUS' strength now failed Him completely. He was near the place where He was to be crucified, but He could not go another step. He fell to the ground, ready to die there. But once again the soldiers forced Him up, and Jesus somehow found the strength to finish His terrible journey.

Leader:

LET us pray.
Jesus,
there are many people who fall into sin
over and over again.
They often feel like giving up,
for they believe that they have no place to
    turn.
Let them see
that You are reaching out to them
to lift them up from their suffering.

All:

JESUS,
You never give up on us.
Teach us to love ourselves
even as much as You love us.
Amen.

Hymn:

O sweet Mother! fount of love,
Touch my spirit from above,
Make my heart with yours accord.

TENTH STATION

Jesus Is Stripped of His Clothes

Leader: We adore You, O Christ, and we bless You.

All: **Because by Your holy Cross You have redeemed the world.**

WHEN they reached the place where Jesus was to die, the soldiers ripped off the robe that Jesus had been wearing. They were going to cut it up into pieces to divide among themselves. But when they saw it was made from one piece of cloth, they decided to roll dice for it.

L ET us pray.
Jesus,
the whole time that they were crucifying You,
they continued to mock You
and to swear at You.
Even now they showed You no respect
as they gambled for Your clothes.
Let us never treat
You or anyone else
with such disrespect.

All:

**J ESUS,
they took away from You
everything You had, even Your clothing.
May we always be willing to share
our food and our clothes and our toys
with those who have none.
Amen.**

Hymn:

Make me feel as you have felt,
Make my soul to glow and melt
With the love of Christ, my Lord.

ELEVENTH STATION

Jesus Is Nailed to the Cross

Leader: We adore You, O Christ, and we bless You.

All: Because by Your holy Cross You have redeemed the world.

THE soldiers then threw Jesus to the ground and began to nail Him to the Cross. They used one nail for each of His hands and one for both of His feet. Jesus felt horrible pain as they were driving the nails into His flesh.

Leader:

LET us pray.
Jesus,
through You God created the whole world,
but now You allowed Yourself
to be nailed to a Cross.
With Your hands You healed the sick,
but now they were cruelly fixed to the wood.
Forgive us.

All:

JESUS,
when we are suffering,
help us to remember that You too suffered.
When we are bored because we can't go out,
help us to remember that You could not
leave the Cross.
When we feel that no one loves us,
help us to remember that You died for love
of us.
Amen.

Hymn:

Holy Mother, pierce me through.
In my heart each wound renew
Of my Savior crucified.

TWELFTH STATION

Jesus Dies on the Cross

Leader: We adore You, O Christ, and we bless You.

All: Because by Your holy Cross You have redeemed the world.

JESUS was crucified at noon and He hung on the Cross for about three hours. Even then, He did not forget His love for us. When the end was near, He looked up into the heavens and said, "Father, forgive them, for they do not know what they are doing." Then He gave His spirit over to the Father and breathed His last.

LET us pray.
Jesus,
by Your death You conquered death
and won eternal life for us.
Help us to live our lives for You.

All:

**OUR Father, Who art in heaven,
hallowed be Thy Name;
Thy kingdom come,
Thy will be done
on earth as it is in heaven.
Give us this day our daily bread,
and forgive us our trespasses,
as we forgive those who trespass against
    us;
and lead us not into temptation,
but deliver us from evil.
Amen.**

Hymn:

Let me share with you His pain,
Who for all our sins was slain,
Who for me in torments died.

THIRTEENTH STATION

Jesus Is Taken Down from the Cross

Leader: We adore You, O Christ, and we bless You.

All: Because by Your holy Cross You have redeemed the world.

AS evening approached, some of the disciples went and asked Pilate for permission to take down the body of Jesus. They lowered Him to the ground and placed Him in the arms of Mary, His loving Mother.

L ET us pray.
Jesus,
Your pain was now ended,
but the pain of Your holy Mother and Your
  disciples
had only just begun.
We ask You to visit those
who have lost a loved one
and to comfort them in their pain.

All:

J ESUS,
we promise that we will now do
what You taught us to do.
We will be Your arms
that give to the poor.
We will be Your feet
to visit the sick.
We will be Your heart
to love all those who are alone.
Amen.

Hymn:

Let me mingle tears with you,
Mourning Him Who mourned for me,
All the days that I may live.

FOURTEENTH STATION

Jesus Is Placed in the Tomb

Leader: We adore You, O Christ, and we bless You.

All: Because by Your holy Cross You have redeemed the world.

IT was now important to bury the body of Jesus quickly, for it was almost sunset. Some of the disciples of Jesus went to a nearby garden and found a new tomb that belonged to Joseph of Arimathea, who was also a disciple. They laid our Lord's body in the tomb and covered the entrance to the tomb with a rock.

Leader:

L ET us pray.
Jesus,
even as Your disciples placed
Your body in the tomb,
You went to welcome
those who had never known Your Name.
We ask that when we die,
You may welcome us also
into Your heavenly Kingdom.

All:

J ESUS, we praise You.
Jesus, we thank You.
Jesus, we love You.
Amen.

Hymn:

By the Cross with you to stay,
There with you to weep and pray,
Is all I ask of you to give.

FIFTEENTH STATION

Jesus Rises from the Dead

Leader: We adore You, O Christ, and we bless You.

All: Because by Your holy Cross You have redeemed the world.

EARLY on Sunday morning some of the women went to the tomb where Jesus had been buried. They found that the stone had been rolled back. An angel told them that Jesus had risen from the grave. The women told the other disciples the good news. Jesus then appeared to them and said to them, "Peace be with you."

Leader:

LET us pray.
Jesus, You told the disciples
that You would be put to death
and rise on the third day.
After completing the work given You by the
   Father,
You now rose in glory.
We adore You and we bless You.

All:

**GLORY be to the Father,
   and to the Son,
and to the Holy Spirit.
As it was in the beginning,
is now,
and ever shall be,
world without end.
Amen.**

Hymn:

Virgin of all virgins blest!
Listen to my fond request:
Let me share your grief Divine.

Conclusion

LOVE, then, consists of this:
not that we have loved God
but that He has loved us
and has sent His Son
as an offering for our sins.

Beloved,
if God has loved us so,
we must have the same love
for one another.